Tried AND True

JOB

The Book of Job for children

Written by Tim Shoemaker
Illustrated by Cedric Hohnstadt

CONCORDIA PUBLISHING HOUSE · SAINT LOUIS

Job got up in the morning,
Had some food, and got dressed.
He had no way of knowing
He was starting a test.

Satan said Job believed
Because God had blessed him.
God gave Satan a chance
To torture and test him.

Three servants came running,
To Job they then said,
"Some bad things have happened.
Your servants are dead.

"There were enemies, an army,
A fire out of the blue;
All the oxen, the camels,
And the sheep are gone too!"

A fourth servant ran up,
"The wind knocked your house flat.
Your kids were inside
And were killed—just like that."

His children all dead.
Now what could be worse?
Oh, what had Job done
To deserve such a curse?

But Job wouldn't blame God.
Satan could not believe it.
So he sent pain with sores,
And no one could relieve it.

Job's wife turned against him,
But couldn't shake his belief.
So Satan wouldn't let Job
Get one bit of relief.

Satan used Job's good friends,
Sure, at first they were kind.
Then they opened their mouths
And gave a piece of their mind.

"The bad things that have happened
Come from sin in your life.
Like stealing, or lying,
Or beating your wife."

Job's friends said,
"Confess it. And do it today.
You must never forget
That sin doesn't pay."

They kept talking like this.
Hey, they got pretty rough.
But God heard every word,
And He'd heard quite enough!
God spoke to Job's friends.

Can't you see their expressions?
"Job's done nothing wrong;
There's no need for confessions."

Job's friends then got scared,
So Job prayed for them quick.
Satan knew he had lost;
He'd used up his last trick!

God ended Job's testing
And healed every sore.
He gave Job ten children
And more stuff than before.

Job didn't understand it.
But then none of us do.
Why bad things can happen
To God's people too.

Job trusted in God
And so passed the test.
God was all that Job needed,
And God knows what is best.

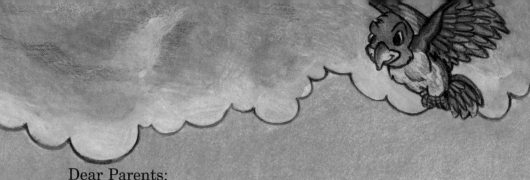

Dear Parents:

God's grace is the theme of the book of Job. Instead of causing suffering in the lives of His children, God uses it to test and to teach. Satan accused Job of being faithful to God only so he could be richly blessed. Satan threw out a challenge: take away Job's blessings and see if he would remain faithful to God.

So God stepped aside and allowed Satan to test Job's faithfulness. Job's wife urged him to curse God, and his friends said that Job was being punished for his sin. Yet Job refused to curse God or turn away from Him. He remained faithful even when his blessings had all been removed. God saw Job's faithfulness and silenced Satan. He restored blessings to Job, not because of Job's own righteousness, but because of His great love.

This story is a miniature example of the struggle between God and Satan, whose efforts were ultimately thwarted through the death and resurrection of Jesus. Satan will keep trying to drive a wedge between God and His children, but faithfulness is ours through the power of the Holy Spirit.

The Editor